THE DAY
the
World Ends

ETHAN COEN

(poems)

THE DAY
the
World Ends

BROADWAY PAPERBACKS

NEW YORK

Ethan Coen is a founding partner
in Mike Zoss Productions.

BROADWAY

Copyright © 2012 by Ethan Coen

Published in the United States by Broadway Paperbacks, an imprint of the
Crown Publishing Group, a division of Random House, Inc., New York.
www.crownpublishing.com

Broadway Paperbacks and its logo, a letter B bisected on the diagonal,
are trademarks of Random House, Inc.

Library of Congress Cataloging-in-Publication Data
Coen, Ethan.
The day the world ends : poems / Ethan Coen. – 1st ed.
I. Title.
PS3553.O348D39 2012   811'.54–dc23   2011052108

ISBN 978-0-307-95630-9
eISBN 978-0-307-95631-6

Printed in the United States of America

Book design by Maria Elias
Cover design by Steve Attardo
Cover photograph: (earth) Kanlaya Naklungka/Shutterstock

10 9 8 7 6 5 4 3 2 1

First Edition

Contents

THE DAY
the
World Ends

We Sheep

We stand across the grassy hill,
The fall line square to each. We could
Chew on and on and on, until
Apocalypse—whose ructions would
But coax we sheep to lift and drop
Our dainty little feet until
The shifting underfoot should stop,
And then we'd square around once more
To crop the newly slanting hill.

Does wisdom fret at what's in store
And boggle at what's gone before—
Or rather does it not, like us,
Do what it must, and nothing more?
And is there credo any know
More sound than that—to just adjust,
Adjust, adjust, adjust, adjust,
And every trouble, worry, woe,
Ignore, ignore, ignore, ignore?

Full Moon

I feel like maybe I'll
Slap my own ass, drop and do
Forty push-ups,
Shit into my right hand, test it with a squeeze,
Fling it out the window,
Fuck the dog,
Yapping along with him, maybe,
Then snap the elastic waist of my undies around my head
    and
Run naked down the street,
Dick bobbing as I scream,
"The big-eyed beans from Venus are coming—
And they're gonna make me president!"
Yeah.
I might
Just
Do it at that.

Regrets

Uh-huh, I loved you once, it's true,
And acted like the man that I
Believed you'd be attracted by—
And I myself believed the lie.
How hard, though, being someone new!
If I'm not him, I guess we're through.
I'm me again—it's sad, it's true.

I loved you once, and that's a fact.
Was it a sin to try to make
A better me for your love's sake?
A dream we weave—but then we wake.
Prince cramps me up; alas, I lack
The limberness to not change back
To frog again—and that's a fact.

What can I say, what can I do?
It turns out I cannot be who
We both can live with, me and you.
The better me was not quite true;
The truer me can't stand to stay;
You wouldn't like him anyway.
What can I do, what can I say?

Untamed Heart

I had a javelina but
It hurried off one day,
Perhaps to join my peccary
Who'd also run away.

The boar I had I loved the more—
Until she too took flight;
I hope my warthog willn't, with
Her darling underbite.

It's true a wild pig will never
Nuzzle you, or spread
Molasses on your balls, or give
You halfway decent head,

But then, its awkward ways only
A pervert would resent,
For in a schoolgirl's uniform
Swine look so innocent.

And so your heart is broken each
Time one abandons you
And scampers off with snuffs and snorts,
Cape flapping, cap askew.

FlashScan System

College Hill Library

Title: The day the world en
Item ID: 33020009511410
Date Due: 10/01/14

Title: True notebooks /
Item ID: 33020007113482
Date Due: 10/01/14

2 items

Date Due: 10/01/14

Title: True notebooks /
Date Due: 10/01/14

2 items

Please return at 5 ... Sunday Tuesday
For renewal information call
(303) 404-5101
Renew materials by phone by dialing
(303) 404-5210
Please have your library bar code and PIN ready

When My Marbles Have Left Me Will You Have?

When my marbles have left me will you have?
When I drool a bit, doze, and come to, have
Some more tea, and then mumble
Of pee as I fumble
At pants about which I no clue have,

Will you check that the pot's not still on?
Will you show me the way to the john?
Will you unlock the door
If I bay in there—or,
When my marbles have left me will you have?

Big-Boned

She was a big woman—
Big-boned; not fat. I
Saw her in a restaurant.
Why should I be ashamed
Of the physical acts I
Wanted to enlist her in?
I am not ashamed!
No one would be hurt, you fuckers
(Unless one of us pulled a muscle,
Which is not what I mean)!
Who would we be harming?
Why not approach her and describe those acts,
And inquire as to her interest?
Why do we live in such a goddamned repressive society?
Why can men not run naked and free
While women recline in the glory of their bodies,
Licking themselves, like cats?

My Epitaph

Why people said of me I was
    Ass-upward
Is more than I can see, because,
    Ass-upward,
Could any man approach the heights
That I did, Glory in my sights,
And—okay, I fell once or twice
    Ass-upward.

Of course my charms would be obscure
    Ass-upward,
But should that earn the nickname Sir
    Ass-Upward?
I spoke not but I knew thereof,
Knelt not but to the Lord above,
And never did receive male love
    Ass-upward.

I swam in Hippocrene clear
    Ass-upward,
And did love you, at least, my dear,
    Ass-upward.
Recall me, therefore, facing thee;
Preserve my ringing poetry;
Forget me not, nor bury me
    Ass-upward!

Night, Then Day

It all takes on a
Yellow cast
When sleep won't come. I read until
My eyes at least want rest, and kill
The light at last.

The bedroom plunges
Out of sight,
Then slowly reemerges, fit
With silver outlines given it
By waiting night.

At length the silver
Turns to gray,
And clothes and chair on which they lie
Are issued back their colors by
Returning day.

I watch the night thus
Stretch and touch
The day. The meaning of the show
Is hard to read. There is one, though—
I know this much.

The Day the World Ends

The day the world ends
There will be the sound of a long, whining fart
And everyone on the street will stop
And look at each other as if to say What
The hell is that
—Til the sound is cut short by
A thunderclap
So loud that,
Ears ringing,
People will stagger about as if drunk,
Hands clapped to heads,
Eyes slit, mouths O-shaped.
And then the vibrating will start—but not last long,
    because
POOM! an outward blast will splinter the concrete
And shoot everyone into the air like champagne corks.
And the g's that suck at their bodies
Will tick down as they reach the apex
Where for one moment they will float,
Looking gravely at each other,
Before starting back towards earth—
Which,
Sad to say,
Shall no longer be there.

And they will fall and fall and fall
With nothing to stop them,
Accelerating,
Faster and faster,
Until they burst into shrieking flame,

•   •   •

And then finally,
And forever,
Their ashes will dither and swirl
In the dusk of eternal nothingness.

When this happens
—And it will—
Don't be saying, "Oh! Oh, wait—can I have a second?
Nobody warned me!"
Try it.
They'll shake this poem in your face and say,
"Remember this? Remember *this,* jackoff?"

Limericks

When their pug began humping his leg
Uncle Vern shook his head at Aunt Peg:
"Can't deny that I've snuck
Her the odd little fuck,
But we can't have her starting to beg."

———

Angry abbess, dull town boy: "Suppose
You explain yourself—*and* Sister Rose!"
"Sorry, ma'am—is this wrong?
All the nuns all along
Have been telling me that's where this goes."

———

O, numbed age! Is there now no more room in
Passion's hothouse for perverts to bloom in?
Any thing you can name
Has been fucked; it's a shame,
But you might as well diddle a human.

———

Mad, the roomers nearby didn't doubt,
Since the bansheelike way she would shout
And her fox-hunting calls
And horse snorts like Huntz Hall's
Drowned the drone of her vibrator out.

———

The don Edmund FitzGibbons-Chase-Lauring
Would declaim odes of Horace while whoring
For his wife had once said,
"Hearing georgics in bed
I find just unbelievably boring."

Then he switched to Greek epics instead. He
Had himself much preferred the more heady
Latin odes, but a bawd
One day snapped, "Oh, good God!
Will you stop with the lyrics already!"

The new form, like the previous one,
Failed to find any favor among
Who as servants of Venus
Could stand a slumped penis
But couldn't abide a dead tongue.

Shun the orotund and the arcane
Then, with wife, or with demi-mondaine.
Though it seems that they would,
Antique words do no good
When the ancientest act is your aim.

———

Any languors that Larry befell he
Quaffed at kangaroo piss to dispel; he
Then got hopping so fast
His balls hammered his ass
And rebounded to bang on his belly.

———

Captain angry at world. Overblown,
Long, digressive, uneven in tone.
Whose dick title denotes
Is obscure, though one notes
Captain's "peg leg" so-called is "whalebone."

———

Deft rebuff: "Yes, it *is* a loud bar;
My place also, though, isn't too far,
And I keep massage oils
That don't sting my burst boils
By my last boyfriend's balls in a jar."

———

After year after year after year
Of seclusion the sage cried, "It's clear!
Yea, all Spirit is just
An expression of lust—
And all Matter should wear a brassiere!"

———

Who can muster a grip with her snatch
Must have mates who perform with dispatch
Because any who linger
Numb dick, tongue or finger
And then must start over from scratch.

———

Old O'Sheen was appalled to awake
To discover the nocturnal brake
On his kidneys and bowel
Had thrown in the towel
To leave him with what those things make.

On Oahu a drunkard named Duke
Who'd resolved to stop squandering puke
Ate the chunkier things
That were strained by the strings
When he vomited into his uke.

———

Stone-age man, thawed from glacier, aghast:
"Was some snowman in my recent past?
And if so, who fucked who?
My dick's numb and quite blue
And there's freezer burn all up my ass."

———

Gavin, given some quivering curds,
Offered grace of a sort in these words:
"Be thou praised and adored
For thy bounty, O Lord—
Not for these mucilaginous turds."

———

Western Lit 101 will review
Basic ways the Great Authors would screw.
Those may learn who so choose
Who ate pussy, and whose,
Next semester in Lit 102.

———

"Do think twice about sex," they said, "when
You're so young"—so we had sex again,
Thinking, Take the thing's measure:
It always yields pleasure,
And progeny just now and then.

———

Though his charm, stoked with lust, could burn bright,
Consummation would snuff it, and flight
Followed lovemaking—or
He'd roll over and snore;
He'd light out, or go out like a light.

This indifference following sex
Would eventually come to vex
His betrothed—and assorted
Young ladies in port, and
A lot of the guys belowdecks.

When a bad reputation began
To thin prospects, on sea and on land,
He fell into a funk,
Then emerged as a monk
With his genitals firmly in hand.

The seclusion's now serving him well,
With the urges he still can't quite quell
Causing no more distress
Since his hand could care less
If he snores after sex in his cell.

———

During vigorous love she would bray,
"Do it, Big Boy!" or, "God! Yes—*that* way!"
"Right in there!" "Right in here!"
—Or else, "Very nice, dear,"
When her husband was in for the day.

———

You may not think to look at her Liz
Performs miracles, but the fact is
She's laid prostrate more men
With her ass even than
Samson did with the jawbone of his.

———

"Set on Low, madame, for whipping cream;
Bread dough, High; or for simply a dream
Of an après-dessert,
Lift your skirt and insert
It and dial it up to Extreme."

———

Of the convent's a hundred nine nuns
Those eight only did not get the runs
Whose insides could congeal
The adventuresome veal
That eluded the hundred and one's.

———

Divine worship in public is bad,
Pat, a Pietist, said—and she'd add
That she cherished the prayers
Of the men who mouthed theirs
In the privatest place that she had.*

*Footnote: cf. the rebbitzen who
Made the case that since nobody knew
Of a scriptural bar,
She could place the shofar
In her person while somebody blew;

Or the chacham of Chelmnitz, who'd do
Some recondite things after he grew
To find intercourse blah—
E.g., have the *sh'ma*
Done in sign language up his wazoo;

Or the traveler only untrue
To his wife with his tallis bag's blue
Satin lining, stained stiff
With shot jissom—"For if
A man screws, he can hardly unscrew."

How contrived are the sins of the Jew,
For his acts file by in review
Under Guilt's parade stand—
Top brass always on hand,
And equipped with binoculars, too.

ETHAN COEN

Greta seethed as she grabbed hat and purse:
Was his grooming or etiquette worse?
How completely low-class—
Finger-fucking her ass
Without trimming his fingernails first!

"They call *me* sick!" the necrophile said.
"It's my partners who lie around dead!
I just like firm support
During sex. Plus, that sort
Of girl stays on her side of the bed."

Oh, the wonderful things I could do
With the energy spent when I screw:
Write, paint, think, get ahead,
And—I almost just said
Even fuck a new person or two.

Wide demand's made the governor sign a
Bill decreeing that North Carolina
Shall have no more state bird
But instead the preferred
(Which would be Anne DeMunn's) State Vagina.

The bill's drafters remade, in their zeal,
The state flag: a raised bra shall reveal
Annie's bosom. A rider
Goes on to provide her
Bare ass shall adorn the state seal.

On the left buttock DON'T TREAD ON ME
Shall be printed; they've yet to agree
On the other: it might
Proclaim FIRM IN THE RIGHT,
Or, if not, then, BEAT THIS, TENNESSEE!

Did it bother Anne having to pose
For the flag, seal, and portrait in prose
Of her privates enshrined
In the bill? "I don't mind;
Without laws and stuff, anything goes."

———

Open-minded, elastically jawed,
And Electroluxlike, Edna awed
All to whom her lips clung
Or who'd hosted her tongue
On its long expeditions abroad.

On returning her tongue to its place
In the mouth of her own charming face
She'd explain, "Out of spit.
Grab that Tupperware—it
Holds the extra I lay by in case."

———

In the annals of ill-conceived sex,
Who's the equal of Oedipus Rex
With his dick down a track
He'd come up ages back—
Reexploring old haunts, in effect.

All our manners and mores instruct
Us in do's and don'ts Oedipus ducked.
Going out on blind dates
Is one thing; when one mates
With one's mother, the family's fucked.

But Jocasta, one hastens to say,
Shares the blame for the plot of the play:
When you will not refuse
To let kids in your cooz
Then you spoil them in the worst way.

The thing cannot but breed complications,
Not to speak of genetic mutations.
Any woman who bears
Her own grandchildren shares
Much too much with the next generations.

———

"Huh!" The city boy, Bobby O'Rourke,
Told by camp counselors it was the stork
Who brought babies, said, "Gee,
Well, out *here* maybe. We
Don't fuck birds too much back in New York."

———

"We are ladies here. Though you may date,
Bletchley girls mayn't entertain late:
After seven o'clock
Students stop sucking cock,
And vaginas close promptly at eight."

———

Though the oral is still ballyhooed,
The Greek anal tradition is viewed
As ignoble now: it's
The rare man who admits
To the act through which it is renewed.

———

"It's your chore, Ella Mae—can't no son
Cure a chaw any good. How a one
Flavors up'n gets warm
In that knothole of yourn
Beats what Abner's ass ever have done."

———

Vikhram clearly expounds on his art—
Advanced Yoga—except for the part
Where his ass clamps his head,
For what's then being said
Slips out just when he happens to fart.

———

Once he'd chalked himself up, Frank Fitzhugh
Would disdain the conventional cue
And could sink with one slick,
Practiced stroke of his dick
All the balls on the table but two.

———

"Sweetmeats Omar" of El Alamein
Wore a turban that asswipes made wane:
He'd unwind what was needed
As restrooms receded
On treks across desert terrain.

At trip's end with his head at last bare
He would pop, to avert the sun's glare,
A silk parasol that
Was as smeared as his hat
From his camel's equivalent care.

("He is sensitive," Omar explains,
"And cloth rougher than this he disdains.
Much is cleaned when one swirls
Upward there, with the furls,
And the tassels pick up what remains.")

Every turd that the beast would let land
Omar kicked soccer-style through the sand
And then sold—dusted white,
And taste-tested (one bite)—
As soft candy, to widespread demand.

All his trips' many hardships and trials
Were redeemed by his customers' smiles.
The concern had to fold
Though, at last, when the old
Camel's anus erupted in piles.

———

The four titles *l'Académie* grants
For distinction in shitting one's pants:
Man of Fiber; of Force;
Chevalier of Ripe Shorts;
And the Hero of Odors of France.

———

Office pool: "Lisa (Bonds) splits the pot
With Mike (Mergers). One taste and both got
What it was and who from:
Larry (Escrow) had come
In the Baggie. Some people guessed snot!"

———

"Anal? Helmet, then. Nothin the matter
With safe sex. Cinch it up. Last wife had her
Nose broke pretty durn bad
In that fall that she had
Gittin some on this very same ladder."

———

"Any openings," Edwin inquires,
"In your person for one who admires
It to such an extent
That for months he has dreamt
Of positions to which he aspires?"

———

"Listen, ye! Music, dance, alcohol,
Women driving, men shaving—all, all
Are forbidden! And hell
Awaits that man as well
Who lies down with a beast not halal!"

———

"Can you bend like a flexible straw?
Have you got a good gape to your jaw?
Will your privates perform
Acts that flout social norm,
Civil statute, and physical law?

"Submit bare-naked photographs, please,
On your back, on your front, on your knees;
On all fours also—but,
If deformed, you know what?
I don't mind if you're down on all threes.

"Great big plus if your wardrobe's diverse—
French maid, stewardess, cheerleader, nurse.
Heidi pigtails are fun,
But not having a bun
Will make slamming the headboard here worse.

"Include measurements—all of the specs
On your titties and so forth. And let's
Hear your hobbies, now, too:
Books you read, crap you do,
'Cause it ain't like it's just about sex."

———

"It's like rodeo," coaxed Anne, "and I'm
Gonna help ever' step. You just climb
On and brace yourself, see;
When my chute opens we
Buck around til our privates clang Time."

———

Dildo language from Legal, with some
Added cautions and comments to come:
FOR INTERNAL USE ONLY;
AS NEEDED, WHEN LONELY;
WASH OFF IF INSERTED IN BUM.

Can we have Risk Assessment advise
About Model XL SuperSize?
Should we warn, SOME ADULTS
SAY DISCOMFORT RESULTS?
Perhaps caveat emptor applies?

Oh—before package art gets too far,
Ed, have Graphics show me where they are
On schematic with slash
Showing danger of crash
Using product while driving a car.

—Nat Black. Brand VP. PS: I'll get
You, whoever the prick is who let
Film of what I surmise
Is the R&D guys
Testing prototypes, onto the Net.

———

"We're a combo. *You* don't like that key
But Elaine has the chorus, and she
Is in F more than not
When she short-bows her twat
While she's screaming 'I Gotta Be Me.' "

———

"Up there, *ever?* Let's think here a bit.
Well, of course, toilet paper. And shit.
Bead things once—crazy date.
If I ain't got a plate
At a party, the odd olive pit.

"Hate to stretch it, though. Story here quick?
Friend of mine tries to jam in his prick?
Biggie, too. Like French bread.
But not crumbly. I said,
'You fit *that* in there, I'll suck your dick!' "

———

Since the lightning hit Ruth Ellen Schwartz
Her vagina gives weather reports
And her asshole intones
All the quotes from Dow Jones
And the scores from professional sports.

As the volume is not very high,
You must hunch at her crotch. Specify
—For she'll stand as you say;
Facing you, or away—
Where exactly your interests lie.

Ruth abides with a great deal of grace
Strangers nosed into this—or that—place,
But her husband requests
You not twiddle her breasts:
Only he adjusts treble and bass.

American Poetry

Edwin Arlington Robinson said,
"Though life brims with regret, loss, and dread,
And its troubles be host,
At least we will spend most
Of the rest of eternity dead."

This, Walt Whitman's take: "What life may bring
I embrace, and of all of it sing
In what sound like moose calls
While I dandle my balls
In its ever-replenishing spring."

Robert Frost: "Without clear way to go,
Life's a path followed darkly, with no
Outcome knowable quite,
Like when tramping at night
To the shitter through deep drifts of snow."

Well: life's none of those things, I declare,
But a one-way and well-traveled stair
Leading deathwards from birth
—Which end hardly seems worth
All the trouble it takes to get there.

Can a poet, though, claim the last word?
As a flourish, once death has occurred,
The deceased may put out
His opinion about
What life was, in the form of a turd.

Got a Problem?

The breeze wafts
Accordion music
From some quaint bistro
Out into the lapping harbor and
Up over the slap and slosh
Of water against the hull,
Then coaxes the wavering melody along the deck,
Ticklingly up my legs,
Through my chest hairs,
And in hurried murmurs past my ears,
While I drink brandy,
Smooth, satiny, twenty-one-year-aged brandy,
From one of those big-ass snifters
In which amber parabolas record sips gone by,
And scan a page of my latest profit statement,
Hand floating to counter the sea swells that gently lift and
    drop
The custom-upholstered deck chair in which I sit
Naked,
Legs spread and heels planted
On either side of a kneeling woman
—Miss America, in fact—
Into whose mouth my dick is slurped
As she sucks and moans, rocking her pelvis
And fingering herself.

I set aside the profit statement
To play with a tendril of Miss America's hair.
She looks up with a damp-eyed expression that says,
Golly! This is some dick!
The scurrying crew pays no attention; they
See this all the time.

They are busy drawing my bath
And preparing my caviar snack, and crepes, and more
    brandy,
For later.

"Oh," you think, "right;
I was kind of believing it
(Because it's possible, after all)
Until I got to that Miss America shit."

Well guess what, jerk-off?
It's true!
I met her in Atlantic City, as one of the special judges
In the competition nobody talks about.

You think this is mere fantasy?
No, you pathetic piece of fuck!
This is my life!
This is how a person such as myself
Passes his successful time!

So I met this broad in A.C.,
Mr. I-Can't-Believe-Anyone's-Got-It-That-Good,
Mr. I've-Got-A-Silly-Little-Dick-And-Can't-Handle-It,
And Miss Vermont (first runner-up) travels with us also
Because Miss America couldn't keep her mouth shut about
    the incredible sex,
And the three of us do this thing now where we
Put Miss Vermont in a leather harness with sheepskin trim
    and
Suspend her over the deck and take a big purple dil—aah,
    you know what? Never mind.
Screw you.
Go read a Billy Collins poem.

Self-Assessment

In his heart a young fighter expects no defeats,
Every ham can play Hamlet, all poets are Keats
And all women are Garbo and men Cary Grant,
Being each of us all his own best sycophant.

Étude

Down
Down
Down
Right Down
   Down
Down Left
Right Down
   Seven O'Clock
 Down
 Five O'Clock   Down Two
   Two O'Clock
Down   Way left
Stop.

What did I just say?

Race

On water other sculls have plowed,
    And leaving just as little mark,
I pull—and hear the shoreline crowd
    Cheer every stroke toward the dark.

New

Bearing on the pinpoint light,
Hunched and speeding against
A headwind that cheek-flaps and buffets,
You peer to the side, nose scrunched beneath your goggles,
And spot it:
Your body/self, speeding on a converging path,
Its comet-tail fizzing in the darkness.
It grows fast, hissing in, and you squeeze your eyes shut
    as it
Slams BANG into your soul/self just at the portal,
And the impact smashes the two of you together and pops
    you out
Merged,
Jarring the breath out of you which you gather back to
    scream
WAAAAAA!
And somebody slaps you on the ass:
"Hello, baby!" Whap! "You're here! That's right! You're
    here!"
Here?—*Where?* And how get used to it,
This space you have been drop-kicked into
Which opens out and wheels away—
Or is it you that turns,
Falling,
In orbit?

Therapy

I went to a therapist complaining
Of depression.
She was a woman
Wearing black slacks and small bright earrings, and had a
    manner
Forthright and brisk. She said, "Why do you think you are
Depressed?" I said,

"I don't want to get old. I
Think about it more and more; it seems even that
My flesh, hanging heavy now, slows me down just so that
I'll have time to dwell on it. I
Cannot do what I used to do; I
Have rounded that midpoint
Towards which Youth canters a-mount eager body and
Back home from which Age leads a plodding nag.
Or put it this way," I said,
"I carry my physical self now
Instead of vice versa,
And it presses warm and heavy on my aching shoulders and
Pours in my ear all its wheezing complaints.
There is no dignity in it;
My body is
A tiresome crone sprouting hair in senseless places
And crying that
If attention isn't paid she'll pack it in—and take me with her.
That's what getting old is and now that I know it
I don't like it,
I don't want it—
How I hate it, hate it, hate it!"

•   •   •

The therapist stared at me.
She stared at me some more,
Then, slowly, she shook her head.

"What," she said,
Enunciating carefully,
"In the name of God's holy fuck
Do you want *me* to do about it?
Am I supposed to tell you
You're *not* getting old?
Am I supposed to *stop* your getting older?
Am I a magician who is going to help you
Slip the gears of time, or would you prefer that I just
Stop the whole goddamn world in its
Cosmic fucking tracks?
Are you OUT
Of your FUCKING
MIND?" (An odd turn of phrase,
I thought, for a therapist.) *"Yes,"* she went on,
"You are getting old.
You *are* getting old.
You will develop
Dark spots as your skin grows
Slack and scraggled
Like the damp rind of an overripe melon, signaling
That you are beginning to putrefy and go
Wrong inside;
You will have
Operations,
More and more of them, and they will become
The focus
Of your miserable existence
For as long as it *has* a focus, because eventually
You will just sit and
Grin like a moron

And drool and shit yourself,
Trembling,
By which point your children—if
You are lucky enough to have children—do
You have children?—will have
Had you locked up in a home,
With some regret at first, maybe,
But soon with little thought of you
Because they will have lives and troubles
Of their own, and you will by then have ceased
Even to entertain with the
Poignantly endearing lapses of
Early Alzheimer's.
And there you will sit, in a corner, staring,
Grinning and shitting yourself and having
Operations, until at last it all gets to be too complicated
    and
They throw up their hands
And pull the plug.
Then—and you will probably be aware of it in a dumb,
Animal way—you will experience
Massive organ failure—
Whatever *that* feels like, but
I'm sure not pleasant—
And will be swallowed by oblivion.
Yes.
It *is* depressing.
So what do you want from *me*?"
—And here she glanced at her watch.

Apparently there was not time for me to answer,
If answer were called for
(And, at any rate, I had none). So
I left,
Strangely comforted.

My Father's Briefcase

His briefcase was a lightish brown;
Its leather tongue would buckle down
To keep his students' bluebooks in.
At night he'd grade them with a frown.

Each morning he would pick it up
—Tongue-tethered thing of brownish hue—
And out he'd go, and blasts of cold
Blew in until the door swung to.

He'd walk it to the city bus—
The leather briefcase, lightish brown—
The bus that was the first of two;
He transferred when he got downtown.

He traveled on the city bus;
The M18 he caught downtown.
He'd spend the day out at the U;
His briefcase was a lightish brown.

He bore a heavy teaching load,
Gave counsel during office hours,
Engaged in research—vexed, obscure—
That would've mocked a lesser's powers,

And got back home with sky full dark
And stew asimmer on the stove.
His coat still gripped the grizzled cold
With which it two times daily strove.

And he removed the coat from him.
The leather briefcase, lightish brown,
Abulge with books afresh to grade,
Would creak as he would set it down.

It rested in the entrance hall
While he consumed first steaming stew,
Then hearty draughts of ginger ale,
And mighty belches did ensue.

The dishes cleared, he picked it up
—The leather briefcase, lightish brown—
And from its swollen belly drew
The pamphlets he alone could sound.

In kitchen light he scratched his marks
In little books whose crackling leaves
We, warm abed, could hear above
The wind that whinnied in the eaves.

Sorry, Pal

Let you out so you can barf?
Sorry pal, no getting out.
The car is life.
Your barf rides with you.

Vine-Covered Verse

No more to roam:
A lorry sped
Him into dust's domain
Who, far from home,
Looked where wont led
When stepping in the lane.

———

When chimed the bell
And slid the door
He stepped, Lord, where there was no floor
And, as he fell,
Abused Your name
Nine stories' worth, upon which shame
His soul—as well
Bereft of craft
Now—hurtled down a deeper shaft.

———

Your passing placed a grievous load
On those you touched, whom you still owed.
Your unearned slumber won't distress
Who knew you more, and lent you less.

———

Lord, keep this farmer's soul in peace,
For, though he dallied with his niece,
And cow, and nephew, none can claim
He, during, failed to praise Your name;
And how commit a lesser sin
When neighbors are but kine and kin?

Adored his wife and how she cooked things,
Batter-dipped and fried;
Grew literally heartsick—his heart
Battered—and he died.

Here, sex's fallen soldier. Love is
Woman's battle plan,
And Comfort friendly fire she sends
Raining down on Man.

His sphinxlike silences intrigued
Us, but the lips once sealed
Have shriveled now from off his teeth
And through their gaps revealed
A tongue that's furring up with mold,
And here, at last, he'll yield
What his head harbored—ripened, now—
To fertilize this field.

Lord, grant this man so often prone
But face now turned to You at last
The grace not there when You were shown
His hairy back and bobbing ass.

Lord, grant this most supine of men
Whose upturned prayers no human heard
The love that he imagined when
He sent his semen ceilingward.

Oh, how he cried
And raised a stink
When things went less than well,
And then he died
—The worst, you'd think!—
And took it. (Though—that smell . . .)

———

A home he never sought.
    He scattered children with his love
            And knew some and not others.
The latter he left naught;
    The former, just the question of
            Just what possessed their mothers.

———

He flossed each day—his teeth were clean.
Each day he prayed—his soul was pure.
Lord, help us know what it might mean:
His soul is gone; his teeth endure.

You, Cow

You
Look at me,
Head swiveling as I walk past,
Making sure I'm not
Anti-cow.

You shit
At the opposite end you eat from,
Body strung between mouth and anus.
It's easy to see
What you're about.

I am less straightforward—
Upright,
With mouth near but not at the top,
And anus somewhere around the middle,
But not exactly.

We are different.
I don't think I could shit
Standing.

Although maybe I could.

I chew
With less play in my jaw.

I run
Less close to my buddies.

I shit
Hidden and ashamed.

· · ·

I moo
Not.

We are different,
So different,
Although not *so* different.

Cow!
Cow!
This is what I ponder
Staring at you.

And you,
Who stare at me?

Each to Each

Feet tramp where trackless snow had stood
And voices ring in failing light
As leaden sky and leafless wood
Await the night.

The voices fade. At length, a breeze
Makes branches dryly creak and sway
As if, alone now, they're at ease.
So ends the day.

In dark the wind as well moves on,
And takes the clouds; now branches are
Dead set, each with a bead upon
Its own cold star.

The men, at home now, by and by
Will kindle fires warm and bright
And bank their growing clamor high
Against the night,

But my friends I dismiss before
Their cheer can warm the night ahead:
Here, bluff goodwill is shown the door,
A book the bed.

The Orgy Ended Late, My Dear

The orgy ended late, my dear,
And this is why I just got home
And why I lack the means, I fear,
To do again what I just did
With Jean and Jacqueline, and Joan,
With Marv and Paula, and their kid
(My goodness, how Marv Jr.'s grown!),
With their au pair, Gret, from Madrid
(Is it just me or is that wrong—
I mean, who brings the help along?!),
And then with some damn person's schlong.
Oh!—then with Liza, on the phone.

And then a bit just on my own.

To the Printer

Why all this white space?
Are these poems such little dears,
Are they so, so precious
That they can't be expected to share a page?
They need
A kick in the ass is what they need.
Then,
Believe me,
They'd sit on whatever page they were told.

Farewell

A horse and wagon bore you here;
We duly filed behind.
The day was dull, the weather drear,
Yet no one seemed to mind.

The preacher's words none succored here
For news of your demise
Nowhereabouts had dampened cheer
—In fact, quite otherwise.

That you shall rest forever here
Is comforting to know;
To meet you was a nagging fear
When you could come and go.

Do not mistake our silence here
For want of feeling; tact
Embargoes sentiment sincere,
Or statement of the fact

That what did formerly inhere
In your cold bones has flown
To precincts past a far frontier
Where cold is quite unknown.

Star

Not an empty seat!
I strut across the arena
Acknowledging all who have paid to see me.
Good people.
I walk before them displaying
The bearing that cannot but please
The discerning eye, and—
Gouch!
What?!
I spin, snorting,
To see a picador with dart-tipped pokes—
One of them now stuck
In my hip-ass.
This bewilders me,
And, frankly, makes me angry—
Who does that!
I scan the crowd, which—strange—does not share my
    outrage.
It roars approval, rather, for this fool who sneaks up snugly
    dressed.
The crowd's cheer, and the fruity man's disdain, lead me to
    believe
The program is not mine.

Okay.
Okay, I get it:
Spaniards.

●   ●   ●

All right then, we will play their game.
We will pretend this is a "contest"
Which I am to "lose."
I *am* the attraction, in any case:
Is not my wreck
The spectacle?

For what is to come?
A poncing entrance
By my flamboyant adversary
Who will sneer,
Give careless cape-flicks that will prick my rage and mock
   it,
Who will whirl,
Take smug steps
Here,
And here,
Who will tilt his head,
Pose,
And plunge his sword
With its absurdly unfair advantage (reach, mobility—
Try these stumpy horns)
To send blood foaming from my mouth
And sever the strings that lock my limbs.

That is what the crowd is here for:
My fury,
My rolling eyes,
My buckling knees,
My neck-twisting flop into the dust.

    •   •   •

The performance will wind down
With the hacking off of my ears and tail,
And the binding of my once powerful, now poignantly
    lifeless, limbs
So that a draft horse may help me exit,
My sign-out a long solemn smear of blood.

Better bull, though, than toreador.

I could never wear that coat.

But, Why?

You stand without
To look within;
To come home, leave;
To end, begin.

I Love You, Said the Man

"If I didn't love you, would I
Do *this*?"
He held his hand over the flame until
The room filled with burning flesh-stink.
"Would I do *this*?" he said,
Pushing shims under his fingernails.
"Or *this*?" he said,
Banging his head against the floor.
"If I didn't love you, would I
Do *this*?"—
Draping one hand over top of his head to grab his jaw,
Cupping the other under his chin, and twisting,
Twisting himself, twisting
With the strength of muscled arms and rippling shoulders,
Twisting his head around until
There were dull crunches inside his neck and
—With a last ferocious wrench and a choked-out
    "Nguh!"—
He collapsed, and lay jerking and trembling on the floor,
Legs senselessly churning as wetness wicked
From his rumpled crotch.

She raised one eyebrow:
"Gross," she said,

Which he did just hear,
And take,
Clattering down with him, to darkness.

Getting Old

Getting old
It really sucks
First goes figure
Then go fucks
Then your wits
Decide they're done
Yeah gettin old
She ain't no fun.

To the English Language

Thank you
For being there
During certain parts of my life:
When friends failed me,
When women dumped me,
When my weight ballooned and I was treated in the
    hurtfully dismissive way familiar to those
Who are fat.
Because of you, I could respond,
Protest,
Declare my humanity
And, in verbalizing, prove it.
Yes, while my weight went up, and down,
While women came, and left,
Taking their record albums and often some of mine,
While certain sores, both literal and figurative, developed,
Festered,
And then popped and faded
Leaving itchy purple marks and memories of pus
(Both literal and figurative),
You were there,
Always,
Giving me a medium for my thoughts,
My precious thoughts,
That nobody else much gave a shit about,
But that I could objectify in you and ponder,
Which was helpful.
Also—
And let's not forget this—
You enabled me to earn a living
And not have to be a farmer, which who wants to be,
Or, worse, forage for grubs and berries as my hair

Got matted.
And you also helped me to persuade women to sleep with
    me
—Women who would later dump me, it's true,
But that wasn't your fault,
Even though some of the things they said *when* they
    dumped me
Were your fault,
In a way,
If you think about it.
But you have been good to me, mostly;
You have let me compare my thoughts
To the thoughts of others down the ages
Who, having been dumped by women and so forth,
Recorded their experiences through you
So that I could relate myself to them
And be succored and inspired.
Also, you will someday help me to recruit new women
(Who—true—will later dump me) to sleep with me,
And plus we can chat in bed after.
So, on balance,
You are good, very good.
You mean so very much to me, O English language,
And I love you.
I love you.
I really do.

Koo Koo Roo!

Eyes open to find—
Dark.

Yes, dark.
And everything is still.

And yet—
Is this not you?
Returned?
Revived?
How strange that it
Should happen so.
But yes,
It *is* you,
Back once more.
But where, exactly? What's in store?

The silence starts to nag at you:
Will all of it come back? Or, no,
How *could* it come back, after all—
The day in all its magnitude?
But—slowly the conviction grows:
It will come back.
It's coming now.
It's on the way.
It's homing in.

Your mind swells with the certainty.
You can't contain what now you know:
It makes your tensing gullet throb
And jams your throat
And makes you ache

To cry what will be—must be—so.
You gather all
That quiet, suck it deep,
So loaded lungs may blow:

"Koo koo roo!"
(Another one!)
The ragged scream
Pulls echo-streamers through the night.
Holy shit!
Another one!

And paling sky
Soon proves you right:
Another dawn.

Your memory
Holds one full day:
Sun coming up
Just like the first time,
Yesterday.
Last night you thought,
When dark came on,
That that was all,
The world was done—
But it returns:
A miracle!
"Koo koo roo!"
Another one!

The lesser creatures
Start to stir.
You strut about, a wild-eyed
Sir Isaac Newton of the yard
Who's linked this day

To that before.
These other barnyard fools have not
The least idea
That all these things
Have happened once,
That all of this
Is Second Time,
Return Engagement,
B-side of Reality—
A half, not a Totality.

You say once more
(No need to scream
With day-again now plainly come),
"Koo koo roo!"
Another one!
Look here. Look there.
It came the same—
You look the whole yard through.
It reemerged
To fall in place
Within the lines
The first time traced.

You pick each place to place each foot,
Each moment for each look and blink,
Each newly scratched-up thought to think;
One follows one of each of those—
Why not Day Two, once Day One goes?
But seed, seed, seed—where's that been put?

At length the sky
Grows dark, and as
Your head descends
To find a wing,

You think, Well, that was that—
And that was just about
The damnedest thing.
How curious
The cosmic ways:
That day should die—
Then dawn again!
That sun and earth
Were granted stays!
O barnyard fair,
Goodbye to you,
Sweet acre where
I lived, times two.
That's all, that's all;
This time it's done;
I'll no more wake
Amazed and make
My fervent call of
"Koo koo roo!"
—Another one.

On Turning Fifty

Having arrived I send back word
On what to expect,
What not to expect,
What to avoid,
What to do.
First of all, don't come here the way I came.
Not through the forties.
The forties are nothing but a good dream gone bad.
I mean:
The deaths?
Not like in your youth when peers' flameouts
—Drugs, motorcycles, etc.—
Little bothered you, or—
Let's admit it—bothered you not at all.
In your forties, the Sad Diers
—From cancers, weird blood diseases, the occasional
       astounding heart attack—
Will give you pause.
These Not-Old who die a-wasting,
Or are smothered by a tumor,
Or detonate,
Leaving stunned young families to pick up the pieces,
Send a message that you now know how to read
And don't want to.
So there's that.
Then, professionally
Things get a little drab:
Doing this, doing that—things you've
Done before.
Sex, ditto.
And just in general the
Idiotic optimism that lit your tripping way forward

Through your twenties and even (if less brilliantly) your
    thirties
Dwindles,
And then one day,
When you're, oh,
Forty-three or forty-four,
It gutters out altogether
With a hopeless *pfft*
And a little spitcurl of updrifting smoke.

So don't come this way.
Skip the forties.

"Skip the forties?" you say.
"Go straight to fifty from—what?—thirty-nine?
Miss ten years?"

Well, yes.
You're not missing anything, is my point.
And once you're fifty
You can start the long peaceful coast down to white-haired
    hardihood,
Wheelspokes humming as age's breeze
Lightly riffles your hair.

Sure.
Why not.

Why
Waste a decade
Dodging the medical lightning bolts,
Why
Sit grumpily
Through the emotional brownouts,
Why

Squint
And squint and squint and squint until you realize,
Fuck! I need reading glasses!
I'm telling you: the forties are nothing.
The forties are less than nothing.
The forties are the ugly stretch of the Interstate.
The forties are taupe.
The forties are ten pieces of shit on a stick.

All right, so this poem wasn't about turning fifty so much
As about your forties, your miserable forties.
But if I'd called the poem "Skip your Forties, Fuckers,"
Would you have read it?

Now that you have—
Learn something, for fuck's sake.
Don't stumble around for a hundred and twenty months
    like I did, blindfolded,
Waving a stick,
And the piñata in the next fucking county.

For fuck's sake:
I'm trying to help you.

Hello?

Legacy

I made a mess
Upon the stair;
I didn't make it to the john.
Do not think less
Of me's my prayer;
Don't dwell upon it when I'm gone.

I've left behind
More pleasant things;
I've touched some people, shown some grit;
Call that to mind,
And sound sad strings
—And careful not to step in it.

The One That Got Away

Something struck me—oh!—and
A poem wafted out like dust-haze when
You smack a rug.
I scurried to collect some words to fix it to a page.
Meanwhile the poem shimmered and
Began to fade.

I rushed and
Bumbled the words I'd
Been putting together and
The words clattered down in a heap and
I bent and paddled through them with desperate hands and
    when I looked up . . .

The poem was gone.

But it was pretty,
That moment that
It floated there.

At Eight Come Do

A dream, a dream,
A honeyed dream:
Throughout the world was known my name.
I was a great authority.
The dream did not declare to me—
    Did not declare,
    Nor did I care—
My field of expertise,
    Nor where
I'd earned my fine degrees.

I lectured here,
I lectured there,
I lectured in a gothic hall.
The audience to every word
Held fast as to the richest gem.
My polished words astonished them.
    The probed and tested
    Insights wrested
From beast Ignorance who, bested
By a mighty Understanding, had been put to flight,
Begat delight.

The rounded words
Rolled out of me.
The lecture's theme I can't recall;
Its echo in that paneled hall
    I can't forget
    (Or haven't, yet),
Nor how the daylight trickled down
To bathe me in my ebon gown.
Yea, leaded windows high on high

Oozed purring sun, beneath which I
Talked on. And on. And on. And my
Face bore a thoughtful frown.

The lecture ended.
Then suspended
Silence clattered down as blended
Whistling and slapped applause
Arrived—effect;
My lecture, cause.
A man with clipboard armpit-clamped
Advanced as everybody stamped
    And cheered. He too
    Was beaming due
To lecture-stimulated joy.
The silken tassel on his hat
Was bobbling this way and that.
With one arm pinching papers tight
He clapped lopsidedly, and might
Have been a windup toy.
    "Good show," he said
    At length, "my boy";
He said, "Good show, my boy."

And in the crowd,
The many stroked
Beards long and gray,
The which bespoke
Not just their years
But that discernment age can bring;
The blinked-back tears
My talk provoked
Effluent from that same deep spring.
"They're moved, the dears,"
Said tassel-hat, and motioned me

To follow. He
Plunged down a hallway:
"Quickly, mind!"
I left the cheers,
And stepped behind.

He hastened, and
I matched his trot.
The hall was long—
A mile, maybe
—Maybe not—
With doors and doors on either side
Of hallway long (more long than wide).
The oaken doors from oaken trees
Had great brass door rings. My good guide
Pulled up at one and jangled keys,
And said, "Just here, sir, if you please.
Here's your assigned
Great oaken door.
I trust you'll find
That this is what you had in mind
As far as lodging goes."
    "Oh, fine,"
I said, "I'm sure it's fine.
The door's nice, heaven knows."

"Yes, fine," I said again, and he
Said, "Breakfast in the Lower Lounge
At eight. Come, do.
Or—I shall fetch you,"
And withdrew.
And I recalled
AT EIGHT COME DO I'd seen engraved
Upon the pediment outside
Where seraphim disported. I'd

Been mightily impressed before
By his acuteness, but the more
I had been given now to find
Urbane the sly allusive mind
Of this smooth functionary who
So effortlessly seemed to find
A way to work this timeless quote
—AT EIGHT COME DO—
So neatly into what had seemed
But pleasantries of little note.
Accordingly, I would devote,
I thought, some time to contemplate
    The motto of this institution—
    Manifestly, that locution—
And its implications deep,
While I wound my way to sleep
Within my bed's belinened keep.
    Or so planned I
    While reaching high
For great brass door ring.
So, inside.

Behold the room:
Bed grand, with large silk canopy,
Emitting squeaky chirps as three
Bare naked women bounced thereon.
They bounced in synchronicity.
They beckoned me.
They beckoned me.
Three naked women.
Of me, one.
I stood entranced, transfixed, undone.
Six breasts—thrice two (I checked the math
By counting, too)—
Each lingering in freighted lag

At bounce's bottom,
Wobbling,
Ere being whipsawed up again
To linger high—and tarry well
Past when impatient earth impels
Her other objects back to her—
Or so it seemed.
     Can bosoms flout
     The laws laid out
By Isaac Newton? Those, though deemed
The highest laws, are not, in fact,
However highly they're esteemed.
Or so it seemed at eight come do.

The breasts scooped out a space-time dent,
Or time-lapse half-pipe if you will,
With rounded walls
And nipple-trough.
(I mentally
Give modest cough.)
At eight come do the women bounced,
Bounced, bounced, the three
One moment earthbound, then, earth-free,
From cushioning to canopy,
Six orbs slung epicyclically
First down, then up, to apogee.

I stared, absorbing more and more
Of that idea
The bosoms seemed to argue for:
Lo, pulling's ever overtaken,
At some point, by being pulled.
My eyeballs tracked. The rest of me,
Immobile, mulled.
The breasts, though unconstrained, obeyed

That law which ever alternates
All playing-out with taking-up.
Life skips a rope
Which, high, is hope,
And, low, is weight;
The two equate,
For hope pulls weight
Til weight drags hope.
    The swinging state
    Instantiate
        In these six breasts
        Obtains no less
In other things—*all* other things;
The law is limitless in scope.

At eight come do. Or,
I SHALL FETCH YOU:
Whence its strange, familiar ring?
I SHALL FETCH YOU:
Name perhaps of Tartar king?
I SHALL FETCH YOU.
I SHALL FETCH YOU.
Aromatic root?
AT EIGHT COME DO or
I SHALL FETCH YOU—
Words that spur—and slip—pursuit.

The lagging mind, though, shall be fetched,
And that will lead that once was led.
Bounce on, ergo, upon the bed
Where beckoned beckons in its turn.
Come too, at eight come do, to learn
    To see the shore—
Where seething water
    Slides from land

And fetches back, in cycles, and
Rewrites the last wave's sinuous
High-water line upon the sand—
As one more place where you'll
Find trailing overtaking—the
    All-present rule.

My bold conjecture,
New-seen slant,
Fresh decoction
New-decant
From Mind's alembic and retort
Would be the stuff of my next lecture:
Deepest Truth eschews support,
Scorns buttress, baling, strut or stay.
With logic's corset stripped away
Three women may—and then, re-may—
Write loops-in-air, as oceans draw
And redraw S's on the sands.
Bound meets Rebound,
For only what is stilted stands.

Before my theory could mature
There came a knocking at the door.
In trotted, bearing brimming ewer
    And enamel basin,
The functionary—mortarboarded
And berobéd, as before.
But why his smile fixed—or did
He grimace rather? No: he slid
His lips back further now to bare
His molars—foil packet clenched
    Between—and there,
    With spear outthrust,
A Trojan soldier, spittle-drenched.

A sideboard served as surface for
The washing things, set side by side,
And, hands now free, my faithful guide
Plucked from his mouth the packet and
    Was poker-faced again.
He murmured, "Cheers; precautions," handed
Me the packet, hiked his robe
And cocked his hip to pull a creased
Red scarf of open-weave batiste
From back left pocket. Snapped out full
And swept upon the bedside lamp,
It served as tinter. My man bowed:
"Well, carry on;
Three's not a crowd,
I shouldn't think—
    Nor four?"
Tight nod, nose tap and knowing wink,
A heel spin; out the door.

The bevy's bouncing, in the glow
Of reddened lamp, appeared to slow,
And, with His Elegante gone,
    I somehow seemed to know
That though I didn't know it yet
    I would know this in time:
I was asleep—but shortly from
This clinging dream I'd climb,
Mind sopping with retained sleep-slime,
Up, up the shore of wakefulness,
Up, even as sleep ebbed behind.

And so, with sigh and stretch of limb,
I rise, embuoyed, and I swim,

And, wiggle-kicking upward through
    The tug of sleep
    To find my feet
On morning's shingle grim,
    I leave behind
    The things not of
    The waking world—
The hallway, doorway, room inside,
The robed and mortarboarded guide
    Who, gone, is with me yet,

And ever shall be so, since we
Are same and one the, I and he.
We both shall fetch me when my dreams
Shove off again from Life's near shore.
Life, overtaking, shall give more
To dream about. The tide that's out
Shall come back in,
And back in comes EC (that's me)
When what was bound, is bounced, instead—
At eight come do.

On Seeing Venice for the First Time
(September 2, 2005)

Seeing Venice for the first time really makes a guy sit down
    and think.
Boy, you think.
Boy, this Venice.
All this.
This Venice.
Wow.
Been here a long time.
Water lapping stone steps.
Doges.
Et cetera.

Then me.
In my khakis.

Permanence.
Impermanence.
(Kind of dank.)
Whole human thing.
Venice.
Gotta think this through a minute.
Man.
Venice.

Can You Explain?

Can you explain?
I don't know why
I sometimes want
To sit and cry.

It's not the sun
So late and low
(You say it's pretty;
I don't know);

It's not that it
Will soon be fall;
The broken shadow
On the wall;

Not end-day sounds
From down the street
Of laughter, shouting,
Children's feet.

Just what it is
Just isn't clear.
It's not what's missing,
Not what's here;

It's nothing I
Want different. I
Just sometimes want
To sit and cry.

Sheep

The gods flung them splat against the hill
Where they stuck,
And started grazing.
The gods, agiggle, let fall back the curtain of sky:
"Stupid sheep!" they tittered.

Even still, every so often,
A god, mood impish, will yank back the sky
To chuck another.

Tee-hee!
Stupid sheep!

Easy . . .

You rise
To dump a paw on either shoulder,
And my body steadies as you let loll
Your great rough tongue.
You solemnly drag it up my face,
Which makes me laugh: "Stop," I say
As your tongue wobbles up into your mouth and
Flops back out to lick again.
I take one retreating step and
You take two shuffling steps
To follow, focused on the long
Lapping of your tongue.
I laugh again as my head wags
Under a slow muscling lick, but
I no longer quite control my laughter which
Comes too hard
As you shift your paws for better grip,
Not laughing.

The Touch

I touched her in a way I thought
  Was it advanced
    In too much haste,—
That she would like, but she did not.
  —The touch that laid
    My prospects waste?

It was a spot a lover knows,
  More widely furrowed,
    Pressed upon;—
And newborn also, I suppose.
  —A sea scent brings
    Its mem'ry on.

But we *are* lovers—or, we were
  Love's locus has
    Too soon become—
Until my touch offended her.
  —An Eden I
    Am banished from.

The spot was *there*—yes! that divan!
  The nearby sea
    We'd hark to on't;—
The touch was *this*—to hold her hand!
  —Its cushions cleft,
    Our happy haunt.

Her hand recoiled. Her swaddled niece,
    Wee chaperone,
        Our innocence—
Placed in between, dozed on in peace.
    —Shall need no more
        Your vigilance!

In anger heaved the bosom I
    Love spurns who courted
        Her for years;—
Cannot touch either. Let me die!
    —Lamented much,
        She disappears.

Repented touch, now paid in tears!
How ill you understood me, dear!

The Word Is Not the Thing

The word is not the thing.
It stands beside the thing
And throws an arm around its shoulder like they are pals,
    while the thing,
Uncomfortable,
Leans away.
Beauty is unself-conscious.
"Beauty" twists a finger in its dimpled cheek.
"The world" cannot quite get its arms around the world.
"The whole wide world" tries harder, flapping its arms for
    flight as it lumbers across the page
Like a goony-bird.
Pain hurts.
"Pain" doesn't.

Writer, ride with the horses.
Don't hang back
With the artillery
To peer through a glass, range-finding:
Aim, fire, look . . . adjust:
That did not—quite—hit it.
One more adjective to the left and
We'll blow it to smithereens.
No!
Don't aim better—stop aiming!
What are you doing?
Measuring your word against the thing?
Dummkopf!
Ninny!
Fleafucker!

A poem is not about things.
It is a thing.
The one thing in which
The word is the thing.

Smart

They hurl their lightning bolts at me.
I duck—and dodge—and feint—and flee.
The great contend; the mighty strive;
The slippery, like me, survive.

Children

One's happiness to theirs is hostage—as if
One's ration wasn't small enough before
Their advent. Oh, children! sharpening
Your cares and woes to arrowpoints! Yes, yes,
Your father knows they aren't aimed at him
But blindly seek who most they will undo—
Just like your love, which he's accepted, true.

Cards

There's little left
Of Cutler's guts,
Wolf-gnawed-upon,
And pecking birds
Have popped his eyes
To get at brains
And headly gore.

Was Moss it was
That done him in.
They'd been at cards
And Moss's soured;
Not Cutler's. Chance
Was not the cause
—Or so Moss swore.

The two men drew
And we fell back.
The two guns barked.
The gunsmoke rose.
We couldn't tell
Which man was hit
As Cutler swore,

For neither moved.
They sat and glared
Each man at each
While Cutler cursed.
The growing stain
We noticed then.
—Then, not before.

ETHAN COEN

98

You, damn, and dog,
The good lord made
His final words.
We gathered round
To check his sleeves:
Two arms were there,
And nothing more.

Moss looked at that,
And looked at us.
A fluke, he said.
The man was known
To hide away
A card or two,
Or three or four.

He sat there, though,
Until the sheriff
Came for him.
In two weeks' time
The circuit judge
Rode in and squared
What was in store.

"Goddamnit, Lord,"
We heard Moss say.
The floor was sprung.
In quiet creaked
The twisting rope.
A whimper rose
From Moss's whore.

Well, Cutler had
Been known to cheat.
No grave for him,
Nor eulogy,
While Moss we stowed
With pretty words
And prayers galore.

Yes, him we liked—
But we respect
The given forms.
And also, who
Begrudges Chance
Her whimsies? What
Would cards be for?

Retreat

The little invalid in here
Is me, tucked happily in bed,
With water glass and tissues near,
Inside the sickroom of my head.

When I my eyelids leave ajar
A visitor sometimes peeks in,
But cannot see in very far,
And that's the way I like it. When

They go away I drift, and doze,
And waking words cannot begin
To tell how sweet the dreams that close
Around me as I snuggle in

To my own warmth. Here, underneath
The coverlet, how close the air
That I alone breathe, and rebreathe.
Outside, I've heard, you have to share.

A New Poem!

I can feel it,
A new poem
Stirring in its lair,
Roused from slumber by
The whipcrack of a fresh idea.
I can hear it, hear
Its echoing moans, and
Imagine it
Unfolding and stretching mighty limbs and
Blinking mucus from its glittering eyes.
Yes, a big'un—
Oh, you can just tell.

Hail, poem, think I
As I feel it rolling to its feet and
Taking its first unsteady steps
Inside my head;
Hail, great grand baying
Awe-inspiring verse of mine,
Finding your balance,
Readying to lumber forth from deep gestation-cave,
Eager to thump your chest and
Stomp fearlessly across the page.
Hail, high howling thing, whose footfalls
Now draw nigh,
Hail to thee, magnificent—

Bald chicken?

• • •

Out,
In the daylight of full consciousness,
Made visible in words,
It pauses and
I look at it,
Aghast.

Is *this* what I awaited,
More ungainly even than ordinary fowl,
Bones a-knock beneath pale skin?
This be it? And what
In the name of all that is holy
Will it . . .
Do?

The bald chicken,
Glistening, feather-plucked, beak the color of old toenail,
Poses at the cave mouth as if expecting praise.
It stares.
Its neck twitches once,
Twice,
And then it decides to strut. It
Clomps about,
Head snapping odd-angled salutes,
Each stamping step
Triggering slack afterflop from
Comb and wattle. Its
Knee-bunched skin, its
Flaccid flesh, its
Stupid blinks and
Jerking puzzled looks about
Commend it not.

●   ●   ●

The bald chicken emits a quavering *squawk*.
No longer amplified by resonating cave the
Thin sound snags on air. It rips a ragged piece away
And flutters feebly off.

A second squawk—
And weaker still.
Eyes bulging,
The creature tries to unhook its sickly gurgle
From the public world,
And the whole sad sound
Retreats back down
The bald chicken's throat.

The throat twitches in distress and
The bald chicken expectorates one last
Blick-squawk that rattles with dismay.
The baggy, stippled bird
Bobs its head as if
Seeking the source of this hideous sound
(Cowardly disavowal)
And then, ejaculations finished
(And blame-laying abandoned),
It turns.

A thinking moment.

Then
It herky-jerks back into the cave—
One final ass-hitch leaving behind a
Slimy
Gray-green
Turd.

And that, as they say . . .

. . .

Is that.

Stunned,
I sit.
And will sit, I guess, and wait for another poem to emerge.

What can you do.

Nimble

You have set out all your glue traps
I have skipped across the floor
I have not stepped in your glue traps
I have made it out the door

When you talked about The Future
I made sure to hold my tongue
When you led with Deepest Caring
I would counter with Good Fun

When you reached for things to bind us
I had whimsy up my sleeve
Which will slick the knots of need so
One may laugh them off and leave

You may call my triumph empty
You may say my life is bare
But that's just another glue trap
And I amn't stepping there.

To a Moth

Thou,
Gad,
Dull bumper-against-screens,
Sun-shunning son of night,
Solemn parodist of flight,
Lurcher,
Lunger,
Candidate but for your size for
Booby hatch or Breathalyzer;
Sluggish climber of the curtain,
Ends unclear and aim uncertain;
Tacker,
Shifter,
Fitful drifter,
Wobble-walking awkward lifter-
Offer, scribbler on the air;
You, errant wafter here and there, in
Euclid's space are not at home.
Non-bee-liner, disposed to roam
On planes unflat, down lanes ill-ruled,
In rules of order little schooled,
Your looping circuits seem confused
And you to your own self unused.
And then: this mix
Of fur and flight—
Can that be right?
One wonders, too:
Since, after all, there are butterflies,
What afterthought, what queer surmise
In God's great mullings brought forth you?
Why one more flitter?
Who needs two?

And do not Darwin's theories doom
The less aligned?
And are you bitter?
Do you mind
That you, moth, are
Less suave by far,
The drabber bug, the
Lesser light?
What slug asleep in chrysalis
Engaged in metamorphosis
Is dreaming he'll burst forth as—this?

Travel Broadens

I must mention that one time while hiking
In the Andean peaks of Peru
I was given a start by the rat-a-tat fart
Of a woolly alpaca there who
Said, "I'm mortified, sir. From this slip don't infer
This is something I commonly do."

I was later—again on a clamber,
Although this time in distant Tibet—
Nearly blown off the track by the fart of a yak
(As farts go, they're as bad as they get).
The beast, seeing me, groaned: "I thought I was alone;
Do accept my sincerest regret."

Later still, at a lecture in Paris,
The professor let something unclench
That let howlingly loose matter much less abstruse
Than the theme we'd expected. The stench
Proclaimed someone from France had blown chunks in his
    pants.
He sniffed: "It is allowed for ze French."

Yes, I've traveled the world and discovered
That the feelings farts foster are apt
To quite widely diverge; telling moods may emerge
When one's innermost regions are tapped
—Though a snob may just want to appear nonchalant,
Even when he has borderline crapped.

Perspective

Below are pluming clouds; below
Them, roads and patchwork fields.
Whenever I in airplanes go
I see a truth revealed:
Lord God prefers soft edges;
He hazily defines,
While men square off the hedges
And travel in straight lines.

ETHAN COEN

What Do I Want?

What do I want? What everyone wants:
Love and a fuck.
What do I need? What everyone needs:
Love and a fuck.
What do I get? What everyone gets:
Love so-called and okay a fuck but then a lot of goddamn
   bullshit.

No Exit?

Birdsong outside mocks the fly
That sizzles round the room.
Help help help help help help, it says,
Indoors is doom.

It rattles between glass and blind,
It bumps the door's high pane.
Help help help, I'll do anything
Except remain.

Next day a creeping square of sun
Finds on the floor, legs-up, the fly.
The gods look down,
And—this is why

They're gods—see cause to smile.
The seeking thing had failed to spy
The window open all the while.

Woman

I was sitting at my desk writing
When Woman appeared.
"You write," she said, "and write and write and write,
But what you write is worthless
For you have ignored *me*."

"Ig*nored* you?" I said. "Ignored *Woman*?
I have spent my entire life thinking about Woman—
Or sometimes trying *not* to think about Woman,
Which itself is hardly ignoring her.
I have honored Woman;
I have feared Woman;
I have groveled before—"
"Silence, little man!" roared Woman,
And the windowpanes rattled.
"What you describe are your own feelings merely.
You have not delved deeply into Woman.
You have not learned—"
"I *have* delved deeply into Woman!"
"That is not what I mean!" thundered Woman,
And the windowpanes rattled.
"You have lain with but not learned from Woman,
And in fact know naught of what She is.

"You imagine
That Woman is a dense body of water
Which you peer at through a rippling skin,
Something composed of forces dark, deep,
And unknowable.

"You believe that you are definite while She
Is wavering mass

That can either bear you up (Good Woman)
Or bear in on you (Bad Woman) until your eyeballs pop out
    and
Your skull crumples
Like an old tin can.

"You think Woman is
A thing you cannot touch however much She touches you,
And that though you immerse yourself in Woman
You know surface only—
A membrane that gives but never breaks.

"She envelops you,
So you think,
Making you spaghetti-limbed and helpless,
She being—so you believe—
An unholdable essence
That keeps your own will
From flowing freely into the world."

"Well," I said, setting aside my pen,
"Isn't She?"

Woman stared at me.

"Yes," conceded Woman;
"Yes She is.
But She is more than that.
Listen to me, little man,
And I will tell you what Woman is—
Not as She appears to you, but as She is in Herself.
Woman is—"
But here Woman fell silent,
Head cocked,
Gaze adrift,

As if harking to a distant voice,
Though I heard only wind.
"Wait," said Woman, urgently,
And then, "Wait."
And then, "Wait . . ."
Moments passed.
Woman blinked, then looked at me.
"Tell you later. I must go—
There is someone else I have to yell at."

Elegy for a Waterbug—and Ourselves

What?!
You're bigger than a bug by rights should be.
I find I cannot smash you with a shoe;
Your shattered shell I couldn't bear to see,
With all your innards squashed outside of you.

Nor can I stomp—and feel that crunching give
Of what you are, while hearing the *crack-splat*
That says that something tough has ceased to live.
Bug-splintering just isn't where I'm at.

I grab the Culture pages of this morning's news.
You flee bare left-hand feints and scuttle right
To patter onto theater reviews.
You pause, antennas paddling for sight.

I raise the paper, bear you off. You stand
Your perch: My john-approaching prayers are heard:
You never think to rush my holding hand.
My wrist-snap sends you toilet-waterward.

What?!
You scramble, manic Jesus on the sea,
And meet and start to scale the toilet wall.
Aghast, I press the lever that will be
The trigger for a lethal waterfall . . .

What?!
You hang on, seasoned tar in sideways seas.
The swirl abates. I, fighting panic, tear
And ball some toilet paper. Fill, tank, please!
When you resume your climb I am prepared

To bat you back in water—thus! You pause,
Afloat, the tank-hiss telling you there's time
To ponder your next move—although, because
Of surface tension, I know that if I'm

Now quick enough to unbunch balled-up wad
Of toilet paper to restore its length,
And drape it onto you to make a sodden
Shroud, a sheet to sop your insect strength,

You may be pinned until the tank is full,
Then flushed away. So I undo the ball
And lay the sheet down, making you a dull
Dark shape beneath, where, finally . . . you stall.

What?!
You jerk to action, scoot from under—oh,
Fierce light that will not see itself unlit!
Life-force insisting it will never go
Where life is not! When you emerge, though, it

Is not on bowl-wall side; you, rather, meet
The open water, mid-bowl, so I may
Re-pull, re-tear, re-lay a second sheet,
And straiten you anew—for, anyway,

What time the tank still needs. New flush; you are
Now swirled out of your cloak and past the bend
Of porcelain beyond which, though not far,
No mortal thing can see and live—the end

Of pawing life! We'll each leave thus, it's clear—
By twirling gaily, gaily down the drain.
Who leaves seems to himself to disappear;
Who stay on hear the crunch, and see the stain.

Pæan

Oh yes you have a whole lot of ass, woman,
Oh big-ass woman,
And you sling it down the street walking, walking your ass, your
    own ass and no one else's,
And it rolls and thuds along, twin crumpling beach balls,
    clomping rear tires,
Flip-flopping ass, walk-slamming ass, wham-bam ass pile-driving
    footstep after footstep, left foot, right foot, grand ass aflop,
Great slaloming ski-mountain of ass, oh big-ass woman, presider
    over two houses of ass;
Ass that clings to you, clings close to you,
Tubby hobo hugging at your hips, ride-hitching vagrant, hauled
    up and around, up and around, ongrabbing bum
Unwilling to clamber down from you, oh doting ride-giver,
Ass-devoted woman, ass-spoiler, woman ass-adored, Great Ma
    Ass,
It yours and you its, it your ass alone in all ass-plenty, it of you
    oh flop-ass tender;
And dutifully you bathe it, daily do you bathe it, sweetly bathing
    it you,
Rubbing and chafing it with nubby washcloth, oh big-ass woman,
    until it is rosy,
Until an Old Master could paint it reclining upon a flung drapery
As you turn back to regard the viewer,
Confirming that this ass is your ass, big-ass woman; yours this
    ass in its assness;
And lovingly you scrub it
Until it fairly purrs with well-being,
Until it shines and glistens and purrs;
And too do you feed it, oh big-ass woman, you pamper it and
    feed it;

Pastries you feed it, through your mouth you feed it, you feed
  your ass, your jungling ass;
Through your mouth you deliver brioche and pound cake and
  fresh whole milk by the pitcherful,
Eating and eating, ass-catering,
Maintaining it in its plumpness, its bigness, its whole-lot-of-
  assness;
And you let your ass drum out that which will not do; you
  indulge your ass, fine finicky ass;
It calls up to you and you heed it, ass-doting woman, lady-in-ass-
  waiting, madam who to ass-muttering harks;
From it you peel satiny undies; down from it you shimmy the
  undies, down;
And you tense your knees as your ass sinks slowly;
Slowly over the toilet seat sinking it goes,
Hesitant, as if led by cane taps, your blind asshole-eye
Seeking its target, easy-kneesy, spaceship to space-station,
  vectors aligning,
Touching down, oh big-ass woman, ass touching down like
  featherlight bird on slender branch and bobbing,
For, woman, you now ass-dowse, seat-tapping, riding seat-
  centering ass-bobs, seeking true toilet south,
Until, ass square, you relax your knees, sending all weight
  assward, full down ass amain,
Blotting toilet seat, ass locking in with sticky ass-upon-porcelain
  seal, oh lady ass-alight;
And from it you issue pounding defecations, oh big-ass woman,
  ass-ass woman, woman lumbered with ass;
Your rimstuck ass pounds away;
Artillerylike it roars and whines and sizzles,
Smashing fecum upon the waters;
And this is it,
Oh big-ass woman,
This is it,
The meaning of ass.

Nonplussed

Who is this newborn,
    Time will tell;
The old man dying
    We know well.

For who departs we
    Fit goodbyes;
How greet, however,
    Who arrives?

The Sign

"No Loitering"? It just occurred
To me I've done it, and in fact still do.
Abashed, I'm newly spurred
To find a mission. If I knew,
I contrived before to keep it out of mind
That failures on my part to go

Someplace must stay within my own home's walls
Lest I impede the buzzing to and fro
Of other people. Gosh! Now it appalls
Me, looking round, that I alone here show
No purpose, while with hard and blind
Determination to get *some*where right away

The passersby push past me. Should I bow
To a random rusher-off and say,
"I'd like to lend a hand somehow,
If you could use one. I can't stay
Here idle, I now know, but home I'd find
No business either, but to sit. And stare. And blink."?

No: surely, almost anyone I'd stop
Would (cityfolk!) just gape—or even shrink
From me. I *could* move someplace less built up
Whose intercepted natives—though they'd also think
I'm daft—would charmingly help *me,* or try to. Mind,
In such a place they wouldn't post the sign.